HAUSA

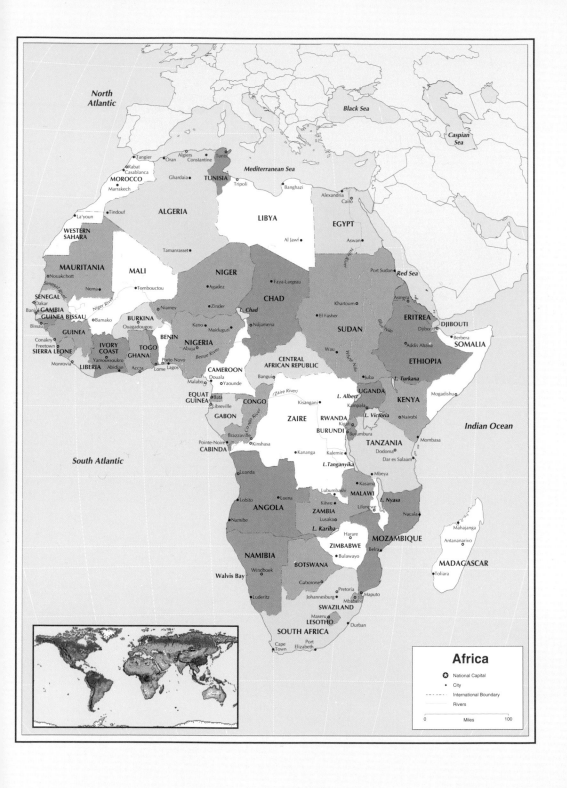

North
Atlantic

Black Sea

Caspian
Sea

MOROCCO
Tangier
Rabat
Casablanca
Marrakech
La'youn
Tindouf
Ghardaia
Algiers
Oran
Constantine
Tunis
TUNISIA
Tripoli
Banghazi
Mediterranean Sea
Alexandria
Cairo

WESTERN
SAHARA

ALGERIA

LIBYA

EGYPT

Aswan

Al Jawf

MAURITANIA
Nouakchott
Nema

MALI

NIGER

Tamanrasset

Tombouctou

Agadez

Faya-Largeau

Port Sudan

Red Sea

Asmera
ERITREA
DJIBOUTI
Djibouti
Berbera
SOMALIA

SENEGAL
Dakar
Banjul
GAMBIA
GUINEA BISSAU
Bissau
GUINEA
Conakry
Freetown
SIERRA LEONE
Monrovia
LIBERIA

Bamako

Niger River

Ouagadougou

BURKINA

Niamey

Zinder

L. Chad

CHAD

Kano

Maiduguri
Ndjamena

Khartoum

El Fasher

SUDAN

Blue Nile

White Nile

Wau

Juba

Addis Ababa
ETHIOPIA

L. Turkana

Mogadishu

IVORY
COAST
Yamoussoukro
Abidjan
TOGO
GHANA
Accra
Lome
BENIN
Porto Novo
Lagos
NIGERIA
Abuja
Benue River

CAMEROON
Douala
Malabo
Yaounde
EQUAT.
GUINEA
Bata
Libreville
CONGO
GABON

CENTRAL
AFRICAN REPUBLIC

Bangui

(Zaire River)
Kisangani

ZAIRE

L. Albert
UGANDA
Kampala
RWANDA
Kigali
BURUNDI
Bujumbura
L. Victoria
Nairobi
KENYA
Mombasa

Indian Ocean

South Atlantic

Congo River
Brazzaville
Pointe-Noire
Kinshasa
CABINDA

Kananga

Kalemie

RWANDA
BURUNDI

TANZANIA
Dodoma
Dar es Salaam

L. Tanganyika

Luanda

Lobito
Luena
Lubumbashi
Kasama
Mbeya
MALAWI
L. Nyasa

ANGOLA
Nambe

Kitwe
ZAMBIA
Lusaka
L. Kariba

Lilongwe
Natacala

Mahajanga

Namibe

Harare
ZIMBABWE
Bulawayo

Belra
MOZAMBIQUE

Antananarivo
MADAGASCAR
Toliara

NAMIBIA

BOTSWANA

Walvis Bay
Windhoek
Gaborone

Luderitz

Johannesburg
Pretoria
Maputo
Mbabane
SWAZILAND
Maseru
LESOTHO
Durban

SOUTH AFRICA

Cape
Town
Port
Elizabeth

Africa

⊕ National Capital
• City
- - - International Boundary
—— Rivers

0   Miles   100

The Heritage Library of African Peoples

HAUSA

Ronald Parris, Ph.D.

THE ROSEN PUBLISHING GROUP, INC.
NEW YORK

To my family in the African diaspora and continental Africa

Published in 1996 by The Rosen Publishing Group, Inc.
29 East 21st Street, New York, NY 10010

First Edition

Manufactured in the United States of America

Library of Congress Cataloging-in-Publication Data

Parris, Ronald G.
    Hausa / Ronald G. Parris.
       p.   cm. — (The heritage library of African peoples)
    Includes bibliographical references and index.
    ISBN 0-8239-1983-8
    1. Hausa (African people)—Juvenile literature. I. Title.
II. Series.
DT515.45.H38P37   1996
966'.004937—dc20   95-43701
                                            CIP
                                              AC

Contents

INTRODUCTION

THERE IS EVERY REASON FOR US TO KNOW something about Africa and to understand its past and the way of life of its peoples. Africa is a rich continent that has for centuries provided the world with art, culture, labor, wealth, and natural resources. It has vast mineral deposits, fossil fuels, and commercial crops.

But perhaps most important is the fact that fossil evidence indicates that human beings originated in Africa. The earliest traces of human beings and their tools are almost two million years old. Their descendants have migrated throughout the world. To be human is to be of African descent.

The experiences of the peoples who stayed in Africa are as rich and as diverse as of those who established themselves elsewhere. This series of books describes their environment, their modes of subsistence, their relationships, and their customs and beliefs. The books present the variety of languages, histories, cultures, and religions that are to be found on the African continent. They demonstrate the historical linkages between African peoples and the way contemporary Africa has been affected by European colonial rule.

Africa is large, complex, and diverse. It encompasses an area of more than 11,700,000 square miles. The United States, Europe, and India could fit easily into it. The sheer size is an indication of the continent's great variety in geography, terrain, climate, flora, fauna, peoples, languages, and cultures.

Much of contemporary Africa has been shaped by European colonial rule, industrialization, urbanization, and the demands of a world economic system. For more than seventy years, large regions of Africa were ruled by Great Britain, France, Belgium, Portugal, and Spain. African peoples from various ethnic, linguistic, and cultural backgrounds wcre brought together to form colonial states.

For decades Africans struggled to gain their independence. It was not until after World War II that the colonial territories became independent African states. Today, almost all of Africa is ruled by Africans. Large numbers of Africans live in modern cities. Rural Africa is also being transformed, and yet its people still engage in many of their customs and beliefs.

Contemporary circumstances and natural events have not always been kind to ordinary Africans. Today, however, new popular social movements and technological innovations pose great promise for future development.

George C. Bond, Ph. D., Director
Institute of African Studies
Columbia University, New York

Hausa professional musicians perform at a wide variety of events. This musician for the archers' guild wears a headdress of cowries with a hornbill beak over the forehead.

chapter

1

THE PEOPLE

THE TRADITIONAL HOMELAND OF THE HAUSA stretches south from the Air Mountains in Niger to the Jos Plateau in central Nigeria. It stretches westward from Lake Chad to the ancient Empire of Songhay along the Niger River Valley in present-day Mali. This region is known as the Central Sudan.

The term Hausa originally referred only to the spoken language of the people to whom the name was applied from about the sixteenth century. Until then, the peoples were known by the various names of their cities or kingdoms. The Hausa are generally dark in complexion, but their language is classified as belonging to the Afro-Asiatic family of languages. Today, not all those who speak Hausa are of the same ethnic origin. However, present-day Hausa stem from black ancestry that was transformed by widespread migration.

The Hausa, who are widely dispersed geographically, are the largest ethnic group in the Northern Region of Nigeria, referred to as the "far north" or the "Muslim North." The second-largest group in this area is variously called the Fulani, Peul, or Fulbe.

Because the Hausa and Fulani have close ties and are often interrelated, Nigerians tend to speak of the Hausa-Fulani as one group. Nevertheless, some Hausa and Fulani regard themselves as distinct. For example, many Fulani proudly remain nomadic herdsmen and shun the settled agriculture that is typical of the Hausa.

The origin of the Fulani is uncertain. Some believe they are a mixture of light-complexioned Berber nomads and settled black farmers who moved into the Senegal Valley together. Since prehistoric times, the Berbers moved around the Sahara. Of the Saharan Berbers, the Tuareg, whose ancestry is traced to Queen Tin Hanan of Tafilalet in southeastern Morocco, were particularly active near the fringes of the southern Sahara or *Bilad al-Sudan*, the "land of the blacks"—not to be confused with the modern state named Sudan. The Tuareg Berbers divided into northern and southern branches. It was particularly the southern Berbers that intermarried with the black people of the south. From about the 1100s their descendants, the Fulani, migrated into Hausaland and other parts of the West African savanna in search of better grazing for their cattle.

As a result, the Hausa and Fulani have lived closely together, often intermarrying and sharing cultural traits. For example, while the first language of the Fulani was Fulfude, some Fulani adopted Hausa as a second language, thus strengthening their ethnic integration.

Not only did the Hausa receive immigrants from the north, but some believe the Hausa migrated south from the Sahara to the savanna to escape desertification and conflicts with competing ethnic groups, including those among the Tuareg Berbers who were warlike. This movement brought the Hausa into contact with other groups farther south, some of whom gradually adopted Hausa language and customs. Because of the continuous mingling of these various groups, Hausa has become the dominant language of the Central Sudan savanna.

Others view the Hausa as Arabs from Iraq. Still others say that the Hausa have farming, fishing, and hunting forebears on the western shore of Lake Chad. Another view regards them as native to Hausaland itself.

The Hausa's own account of their origin is in the Daura serpent legend. It is said that Prince Bayajida of Baghdad journeyed from Iraq to

Kanem-Bornu. The King of Bornu allowed the prince to marry his daughter but separated him from his followers. Suspicious of the king's motives, Prince Bayajida fled westward, leaving his pregnant wife at Biram-ta-Gabas. Near Kano, he commissioned some blacksmiths to make a sword for him. At a well where a sacred snake was preventing the people from drawing water, Prince Bayajida killed the snake with his special sword.

Out of admiration and gratitude, Daura, the queen of the town, promptly married him and also rewarded him with a Gwari concubine. Bayajida had sons by both of them: Bawogari, the son of Daura, and Karbogari or Karafgari, the son of the concubine. Subsequently, Bawogari had three sets of male twins, who founded Kano and Daura, Gobir and Zazzau (Zaria), and Katsina and Rano.

Another son of Prince Bayajida ruled Biram. These made up the seven Hausa states, or the *hausa bakwai*. In addition, seven sons of the concubine's son Karbogari established another seven states: Kebbi, Zamfara, Gwari, Jukun (Kwararafa), Yoruba, Nupe, and Yawuri, but these were pejoratively called *banza bakwai*, or bastard states.▲

2

POLITICS

THE PERIOD BETWEEN AD 1000 AND 1500 IS
regarded as a golden age of West African development. It was a period of expansion of trade,
wide adoption of metalworking, and the growth
of cities, states, and empires. In southeastern
Sudan, the Hausa states and the Empire of
Kanem-Bornu were the most important political
entities.

The earliest record of Hausa state formation
goes back to the first king of Kano in 999, when
some small settlements grew into cities and states.
They functioned as centers for government and
military protection. They were also places of
exchange for both long-distance traders from
North Africa, Muslim centers, and Europe and
for local farmers and craftsmen. The Hausa states
of Katsina and Kano were the most important
early commercial centers and, together with the

Kano was the first Hausa city-state. This is a view of the old section of the city.

states of Zaria and Gobir, remained powerful up to the nineteenth century. The emergence and growth of states during this period, however, were accompanied by numerous episodes of internal conflict among the Hausa states themselves and with their neighbors. Hausaland never attained political unity until it came under the domination of the Fulani in the nineteenth century. More unified groups, such as the Songhay, the Jukum, and the Kanuri thus were able to conquer various Hausa states from time to time.

For much of their history, the Hausa had two

powerful neighbors on their borders: the
Kanem-Bornu Empire in the east and the
Songhay Empire in the west. The Hausa states
of Kano and Katsina came under the domination of Kanem-Bornu for some time in the fif-
teenth century.

The Songhay, under Askiya Mohammed, also
conquered Kano and almost all of Hausaland in
the 1520s, despite strong resistance by the state
of Katsina. The defeated Hausa states had to
pay tribute and were administered by resident
agents. Some point out that no such event is
recorded in the Hausa or Timbuktu Chronicles,
which are the major historical records for recon-
structing regional history. A Songhay invasion is,
however, reported by Leo Africanus, the Moroc-
can Arab traveler who was in the region at the
time. In any case, Songhay had an immense
cultural influence on Hausaland. The flourishing
intellectual life at Timbuktu permeated the region, and Arabic language and culture spread to
other cities and beyond.

Not being unified, Hausaland was also at-
tacked by the state of Kebbi, when the latter
regained its independence from Songhay in a
celebrated victory at Tara in 1517. Under the
leadership of Kanta Kotal, Kebbi overran the
Hausa states of Gobir, Katsina, Daura, Kano,
and Zaria. Kanta Kotal, regarded as one of the
greatest leaders of his time, established a king-

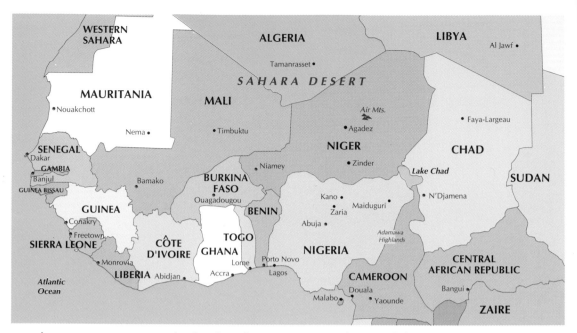

The Hausa states once had wide influence in West Africa and their trade routes led to the Atlantic coast and across the Sahel and the Sahara Desert. Today Hausa states are found in northern Nigeria.

dom with a large army and nurtured ambitions to build an empire in Hausaland to rival Songhay and Bornu.

One of the strongest Hausa states in the 1500s was Zaria, which for some time controlled both the kingdoms of Nupe and Jukun in the south. Zaria rose to power under Queen Barkwa Turunda and her celebrated daughter Amina, who reigned for thirty-four years. Queen Amina extended the territory of her kingdom through military successes.

In addition to external threats, Hausaland also experienced episodes of internal conflict among its states. The 16th-century struggle between Kano and Katsina, for example, was caused by dispute over the control of the southern end of the trans-Saharan trade, by blood feuds between the ruling families, or both. This long and intense battle ended in 1650 when Katsina emerged victorious. It then, however, promptly joined with Kano against the common threat of the Kwararafa or Jukun invaders.

Lasting political union, however, continued to elude the Hausa states, although there were some notable examples of military cooperation between states. Between 1500 and 1800, various Hausa states rose and fell as they competed with each other for dominance. Kano rose to power between 1620 and 1730, and Gobir was at the peak of its power from 1730 to 1808. As the states grew in strength and traded with each other, they formed bonds of language, Islamic culture, and religion that gave Hausaland some form of unity.

▼ MIGRATION ▼

The political turmoil in Hausaland in the 1500s was accompanied by large-scale immigration that continued in the 1600s, especially to Kano and Katsina. Immigrants came from Bornu, the Mali and Songhay empires in the west, and from the Sahara. Among these immigrants were Tuareg and Fulani herdsmen; Songhay fishermen and farmers; Arab, Wangarawa, and Berber merchants and traders; Muslim scholars and clerics; and refugee aristocrats from Bornu. Immigrants strengthened Islamic literacy and learning among the Hausa, especially in the cities.

As immigration went on, the Hausa people themselves were also moving west and south to avoid military threat or follow trade and farming opportunities. Hausa emigration to various parts of West Africa was substantial after the 1500s.

Such population movements, however, had political and cultural risks. The Tuareg, one of the Saharan Berber groups frequently on the move, fought the Hausa of Gobir, finally overthrowing them and establishing their Muslim rule in 1495. The spread of the Arab language

These pages from a Hausa miniature Koran, each about three inches square, show Islamic influence.

and the Muslim religion accompanied such migration and conquest. The Islamization of the Hausa weakened the political structure and authority of local chiefs, who perceived this external influence of Islam as a threat. Local chieftaincies were eventually ignored as state structures became more centralized. Traditional places of worship were deliberately destroyed to remove the chiefs' main focus of power.

The process of Islamization did not completely eliminate traditional religious beliefs either in the rural areas or even among the converted. Belief in other gods, magic, and witchcraft persisted. The impact of Islam was greatest among the ruling elite of merchants and traders in the cities and large towns.

▼ HAUSA POLITICAL ▼ INSTITUTIONS

Early political life in Hausaland was centered on the hamlet or village (*gari* or *kauye*)

Rural Hausa live in small villages. Houses and even beds, such as that seen here on the right, are made of mud.

in the rural areas and on the walled or stockaded town (*birni*) in the cities.

The elementary unit of rural politics was a group of families (*gidaje*) under the authority of a chief. Different family groups lived in small rural communities (*kauyuka*). Villages (*garuruwa*) were larger and more permanent and headed by a village chief (*sarkin gari* or *magaju gari*), who was sometimes assisted by district leaders (*masunguwa*).

The district capital or *birni* headed this hierarchy. Trade was conducted in the fortified town, which was surrounded by farmland. The *birni* was a relatively self-sufficient community. The *birni* itself was headed by a Sarkin Kasu, the district or county chief, who had authority over all the other chiefs.

The head of the country was the divine king or Sarki, who had absolute power over his kingdom. He was normally chosen from the royal lineage of princely families in closely related cities and provinces. The nobility controlled the machinery of the state and maintained their power through marriage to each other. A lower level of state officials was appointed by the Sarki for duties in the state bureaucracy and military. By their position, they gained access to wealth and prestige. Together, these groups constituted an aristocracy called the *masu sarauta*.

From this group was chosen the Council of

Houses in Hausa towns are frequently decorated by professional artists. This house is in Zaria.

Large Hausa towns and cities were surrounded by secure walls like those behind these Hausa horsemen, who are taking part in a feature film.

State. Important posts among the state officials included the *galadima*, who was like a prime minister, responsible for all affairs of state. He was left in charge when the Sarki and other chiefs went to war. In some states he was always a eunuch. Holders of this powerful office sometimes became Sarki.

The *galadima* was served by a number of officials and dignitaries, each responsible for a particular function or territorial unit. Among these officials was the Madawaki or Madaki, commander-in-chief of the army. He was next in importance to the Sarki, served as his appointments adviser, replied to the Sarki's address on feast days, organized the meetings of the chief councillors, and shared responsibility with them for choosing

Hausa politics were controlled by a strict heirarchy of nobles. Seen here is Alhaji Sir Ahmadu Bello, the Sardauna of Sokoto, Premier of the Northern Region of Nigeria in 1959, when this picture was taken.

The Hausa are famous equestrians. Seen here is the mounted body-guard of the Emir of Katsina.

the new king. Other key officials included the Lord of the Treasury (Magaji); the Head Gaoler (Yari); Head of the King's Bodyguard (Sarkin Dogarai); and Chief of Police (Sarkin Yan Doka). Slaves were household servants and laborers, and were used as currency. They occupied a subordinate position in Hausa society.

The Hausa people were renowned both for trading and fighting. The courage and reliability of Hausa mercenaries were highly valued. In colonial times, the French relied on Hausa soldiers to help control their colony of Madagascar. The Belgians used Hausa forces in the Congo. The Germans recruited both Hausa soldiers and traders in their conquest of Cameroon; the former to fight, the latter to act as guides and spies.

The British formed the Armed Hausa Police Force in their colony at Lagos in 1863. The recruits were mainly liberated or runaway Hausa slaves, who joined up to gain their freedom. In Lagos they were given plots of land and became a privileged group.

Hausa soldiers helped the British defeat the Asante in Ghana in 1873–74. A number of Hausa policemen were also transferred from Lagos to Ghana. After the British victory, many Hausa were recruited into the Ghanaian army.

In return for their efforts, the Hausa benefited substantially from European colonialism. Apart from land grants to attract their service, the British built a mosque at their headquarters in Ghana, and granted them privileges to ensure their loyalty. Moreover, the Asante defeat broke the trade monopoly of the Asante between the coast and the interior. Hausa traders could then ignore the Asante ban on their movement to the south and the trade embargo that the Asante had imposed. Many Hausa migrated to Ghana from the savanna belt and spread all over the country. They included traders, Muslim clerics or *malaams*, craftsmen, butchers, drummers, and porters. Prostitutes were also among these migrants. The Hausa came to control much of

Most Hausa are now Muslim. These worshipers are at the Massalajin Bello mosque in Sokoto, Nigeria.

the commerce in Ghana and spread Islam and Hausa culture in the region. Despite the advantages for the Hausa, European colonialism destroyed the military and political power of the West African kingdoms and states.

▼ SYSTEM OF JUSTICE ▼

Traditionally, complaints were brought before the village or district head, or, if in the capital, the Sarki himself. The Sarki was assisted by the chief official of his household and other officials to address grievances. Petty offenses were dealt with by the Sarki alone, but his councillors were consulted on more serious crimes.

The adoption of the Islamic system of justice, *sharia*, brought about a separation of executive and judicial functions. However, the ultimate judge in some matters was still the Sarki. The Muslim system included a professional class of magistrates and jurists trained in the law, with the major judicial responsibility entrusted to the Alkali, who was responsible for administering the Maliki Code.

Judges traveled to local courts in outlying districts, which had the right of appeal to the high court in the capital. In smaller villages, judicial authority was vested in the village head, though minor offenses could be settled by family heads or chiefs.▲

3

ECONOMICS

THERE WERE THREE MAJOR SOURCES OF
funding the state in Hausaland: tribute and gifts;
taxes and duties; and spoils.

▼ TRIBUTE OR GIFTS ▼

For a long time, the Hausa depended on a
system of tribute or gifts in currency (including
slaves), commodities (including slaves), or services provided by inferior individuals, villages,
cities, or states to their superiors in military
strength or social status.

A state that is required to pay tribute to another, or to an empire, is called a vassal of the
superior state. Officials and dignitaries custom-
arily presented gifts (*gaisuwa*) to their superiors
and the Sarki, and they hoped to be granted
favors in return. The value of the gift was expected to reflect the status of the giver, and the

Hausa leaders, such as the Emir of Katsina seen here, hold an elaborate ceremony for making morning greetings.

superior could be pleased or displeased by the gift's value. This system was open to abuse and manipulation.

▼ TAXES AND DUTIES ▼

Islamization introduced a system of taxes and duties on livestock, land, professions (craftsmen, butchers, dyers, prostitutes, and others), and luxury crops such as tobacco, onions, and sugarcane. A "capitation tax" was imposed on conquered people and was usually paid in slaves. On receiving pardon, an offender was required to pay a "forgiveness" tax to the Sarki. Tolls were charged for traveling on caravan routes and for participating in markets. All persons visiting their superiors were expected to pay tribute or *gaisuwa*. Although the levying of taxes fell under Muslim law, abuses still occurred, especially among the powerful nobles. The collection of taxes in the villages was delegated to agents, who sometimes engaged in extortion and fraud.

▼ SPOILS ▼

Spoils, as a source of revenue, derived usually from raiding others' property. Such pillaging yielded a variety of goods and commodities, such as slaves and cattle.

▼ AGRICULTURE ▼

The main economic activity of the Hausa in precolonial times was agriculture. Most Hausa farmed to some extent and supplemented their income by making handicrafts and trading.

In order of importance, the crops were millet, guinea corn, groundnuts, and cotton. The flat countryside was also suitable for sorghum, rice, barley, citrus fruits, beans, sweet potatoes, cassava, wheat, sugarcane, and a variety of vegetables. The Hausa also raised donkeys as a means of transport and goats for household use, including ceremonial sacrifice.

Farming was carried out in different ways depending on the nature of the soil. During the hot season, shrubs were cleared and burned to serve as fertilizer, and together with manure were spread evenly over the land. As the rainy season began, the farmer and one or more of his elder sons dug the holes for sowing. The rest of the family followed, sowing the grain in the holes. After the sowing of millet and guinea corn, the farmers sowed groundnuts. In the south, cotton was sown after the harvesting of millet and was ready for harvesting only in the dry season, after the harvesting of all other farm crops.

Historically, the greater part of the Hausa population lived in small farming villages, though walled fortified towns soon emerged. The land was owned by the community, either the hamlet, village, or town, with a chief responsible for deciding on the rights to use the land. The Hausa relied on the extended family or *gida* and the mutual aid system or *gayya* for their labor. Farming activities were organzed by a leader called the Chief of Crops (Sarkin Poma), whose duties included the monitoring of the seasons and hence the scheduling of agricultural activities and ensuring that the appropriate sacrifices were made to the local gods to assure a good harvest.

Three types of farms were found in Hausaland: the large farm of the king, or *gandum sarkin*, the family farm, or *goma*, and the individual field or *gayaima*. The main source of

labor on the large estates of the king and state officials was slaves.

▼ CRAFTS ▼

Next in importance to agriculture in the Hausa economy was handicrafts, observed by foreign visitors to have been of high quality in the 1300s and 1400s. The Hausa produced textiles and manufactured cotton cloth for much of their history. All phases of manufacture—ginning, carding, spinning, dyeing, and weaving—were well developed locally. The Hausa also produced and traded fine leather goods, including charms, amulets, saddles, cushions, shoes, and a variety of leather bags for storing grain, water, or books. Potterymaking was a traditional occupation passed from father to son. Many articles were made from clay, including pots, basins, and lamps. Metal implements such as farm tools, knives, axes, cooking pots, spears, and arrowheads were all produced locally, with Kano being a well-known center of manufacture.

Activities such as spinning, weaving, dyeing, and embroidery became specialized trades. They were regulated by a system of guilds that represented the occupations to state authorities. Guild leaders were appointed by the Sarki, sometimes on the recommendation of guild members. Their functions included the collec-

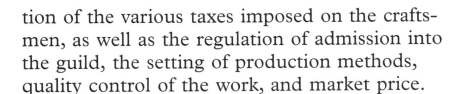

tion of the various taxes imposed on the craftsmen, as well as the regulation of admission into
the guild, the setting of production methods,
quality control of the work, and market price.

▼ MARKETS ▼

The markets for Hausa goods were of three
types. Small farmers and craftsmen marketed
their products at the local trade market, the
ciniki. In the case of craftsmen, customers went
to their homes to buy their goods. The second
type of market was the wholesale market or
fatauci for long-distance trade. The third type of
market combined elements of the other two and
was called *yan koli*. Salesmen went from one
market to another buying and selling cheap
goods, or retailing those imported by wholesal-
ers. The established markets had a broker or
dillali, who kept a careful account of the prices
in each regional market. He estimated fluctua-
tions in demand, supply, and price, for which he
received a percentage of the sale price. For a
long time, such commodities as cotton cloth,
salt, slaves, and cowrie shells served as mediums
of exchange, or currency.

▼ TRADE ▼

Trade, a key sector of the Hausa economy,
consisted of three major types: overseas or external trade; long-distance trade to towns and

countries in the region; and domestic or internal trade within Hausaland.

▼ OVERSEAS TRADE ▼

Overseas trade required access to adequate capital and know-how and was in the hands of the state and large European, Arab, and Nigerian traders. Slaves for the American cotton and sugar plantations came to dominate overseas trade from West Africa, especially in the 1700s and 1800s. West African middlemen and suppliers secured slaves from the vast interior of Hausaland and other states in West Africa and delivered them to Europeans on the coast. Many of these states had already established traditions of domestic slavery and trading in slaves with North Africa and the Middle East. The export trade in slaves was therefore a cooperative undertaking of European and African interests.

The slaves brought into Hausaland came mainly from raids or as tribute from neighboring countries, but the Hausa also obtained some of their slaves from within their own villages and towns. Orders by one ruler for a number of slaves to be paid as tribute to another ruler sometimes meant raiding his own town or village for the needed supply.

Slaves who were not exported to Europe and America fulfilled a number of domestic roles as household servants, soldiers and guards, craftsmen, porters or carriers, and as commodities of exchange when large transactions were involved, such as the paying of tribute. For example, the number of slaves to be taken on a journey would be estimated in proportion to the length of the journey—much like travelers checks—so that their masters would have an adequate number to sell at various stops, finally ending the return journey with hardly any slaves. The price of slaves varied according to age, gender, and demand. In 1896 the price of slaves, paid in cowries, was equivalent to seven to ten English pounds for a girl of fourteen, six pounds for a male of eighteen, and four pounds for a man of thirty, the price decreasing with age.

Hausa masters had almost complete freedom in how they treated their slaves. They could not kill them, but they were free to dispense their labor and dispose of their persons as they chose. If, however, a slave bore a child to a freeman, she could not then be sold. Slaves were allowed to marry each other, with the consent of their masters, but could not marry freemen.

When the overseas slave trade was formally abolished in the nineteenth century, the trading networks that had been cemented by the years of cooperation between European and African traders simply remained open to receive other products, such as palm oil and groundnuts, which finally replaced slaves as chief commodities.

Trade played a vital role in the rise and success of the various Hausa states.
The camel was essential in long-distance trade across the Sahara Desert.

▼ REGIONAL TRADE ▼

The Hausa were strategically located for trans-Saharan, long-distance trade. Situated between the Sahara region to the north and the savanna grassland and tropical rain forest to the south, they were ideally placed to link these distinct ecological zones into a vast market for goods and services and intercultural exchanges. By at least 1,000 years before the present era, a series of caravan routes crossed the Sahara, linking the Sudan to Egypt and other Mediterranean North African states. The southern networks traversed Zaria, Birnin Gwari, and Birnin Yawuri toward Timbuktu and the region of the Yoruba and Nupe. A western trade route crossed the Sahara from southern Morocco to Timbuktu in Songhay. An eastern route led from Lake Chad northward to Fezzan, near modern Tripoli. The states of Katsina and Kano were key points in the Central Sudan on the north-south and east-west routes.

These routes were filled by the goods of a variety of traders: small traders and wealthy merchants both engaged in *fatauci* or long-distance trade. Goods were transported by caravans under the supervision of professional leaders called *madugu*. At first, caravans of thousands of small traders carried loads on their heads or used donkeys as a means of transport. The goods of wealthy merchants were carried by

porters (sometimes slaves) and pack animals.

The volume of trans-Saharan trade is thought to have expanded significantly when the camel was introduced to supplement the use of horses, donkeys, and mules. This trade was immensely stimulated by the Muslim Arab invasion of North Africa in the seventh century, and the large-scale export of gold from the forest belt in the region of the upper Senegal River, the Niger River, and the Volta River. The Empire of Ghana established itself as a crucial link in this trading network as well as in the trade of desert salt and copper. On the routes from Lake Chad, both Bornu and the Hausa city of Kano assumed similar importance from about the 1400s in the regional system of markets. Slaves replaced gold as the major export because of a growing demand for household slaves in North Africa and southwest Asia. In addition to slaves, the Hausa exported leather goods, dyed Kano cloth, millet, hides, and iron.

The Hausa purchased various Arab and European goods, such as firearms, camels, horses, paper, needles, mirrors, beads, dates, cloves, and salt from the Sahara.

With the western states, the Hausa traded mainly handmade cotton garments, embroidered gowns, and leather goods.

Hausa traded with neighboring Ghana, Bornu, and Niamey and with distant Bangui,

Kinshasa, Brazzaville, Dakar, and Gambia. Hausa also forged strong commercial links with the Yoruba to the south. The Yoruba traded kolanuts, palm oil, timber, citrus fruits, shoes, and pottery for Hausa textiles, leather, cattle, sheep, goats, rice, beans, and fowl. In trading with neighbors to the west, the Hasua established small settlements along the routes, such as at Birnin Yawuri and Agwara.

▼ INTERNAL TRADE ▼

The third type of commerce was the internal trade within Hausaland, between villages, towns, and provinces. Markets opened daily at such important trading centers as Kano, Zaria, Katsina, and Sokoto. Historically, this internal trade was also linked to the export of such important products as gold and kolanuts destined for markets in the north and northeast. Mande traders brought these to the Hausa markets from the rich supply in the savanna belt of West Africa, since Hausaland was an important transshipment point for these commodities.

Camels were used to transport Hausa goods, expecially northward from the busy commercial state of Kano. Horses and donkeys transported kolanuts to Hausaland and textiles and leatherware exports on the return journey southward. Hausa embroidered gowns were favored by chiefs in Ghana, whereas other woven gar-

ments were generally adopted and worn by ordinary people.

The Hausa clearly have a strong tradition of trade. Both the commercial and industrial sectors expanded dramatically in the 1800s, as did the spread of Hausa culture throughout West Africa. This development was part of the more general political, economic, and cultural changes occurring in the Central Sudan, including the aggressive religious movement of Islam to all parts of West Africa. All types of Hausa were on the move: religious teachers or *malaams*, traders, craftsmen—especially blacksmiths and textile and leather workers—drummers and other musicians, farmers, elephant hunters, rubber tappers, and refugees.

These changes were ushered in by Sheik Othman in 1802 in what has been called the Sokoto Jihad, a sort of religious war by the Fulani to convert all of Hausaland to Islam. The Hausa fought each other and many religious teachers and craftsmen were sold into slavery. Sheik Othman was finally victorious. With his capital at Sokoto, he established himself as ruler over a large part of Hausaland. When he died in 1817, the empire was divided between his sons Mohammed Bello and Abdellah; the former ruled Kano, Katsina, and Zaria, and the latter inherited the southwestern portion of the empire.

chapter

4

CUSTOMS

▼ **RELIGION** ▼

Islam became the predominant religion among the Hausa. It was probably introduced by Muslims from North Africa, Mali, and neighboring Kanem and was known in Hausaland before the 1300s. Its influence, however, was for a long time chiefly on the migrant traders, merchants, and the local elite in the towns and cities. Generally, Hausa viewed it with suspicion and continued their traditional religion. By the 1400s, Islam was established in Kano and Katsina and was strengthened by Muslim clerics and scholars.

The first successful wide-scale effort to convert the general population occurred during the Sokoto Jihad at the beginning of the 1800s. Then all Hausa kings identified themselves as

Hausa children learn to write Arabic on tablets that can be washed clean for further practice.

Muslim and proclaimed Islam the official religion of their states. Attempts to spread Christi-
anity in the north confronted not only those
committed to their traditional faith, but growing
Islamic influence. Christian missionaries made
an impact in Hausaland only under colonial
rule, mostly in Zaria.

The spread of Islam was closely related to the
migrations discussed earlier, to long-distance
trade, and to the role of the itinerant *malaams*,
who taught and spread basic education and literacy during their travels and pilgrimages to and
from Mecca.

Muslims are expected to observe the five "pil-
lars of Islam": *Tauhidi*, or proclamation of the
oneness of God; prayer; fasting in the month of
Ramadan; payment of alms; and pilgrimage to
Mecca if possible. The Hausa follow the form of
prayer called Sallah, generally similar to the
prayers said by Muslims all over the world. Be-
lievers are obliged to say prescribed prayers five
times a day: at dawn, two o'clock in the after-
noon, four o'clock, dusk, and after dark. Muslims should purify themselves before prayers by
taking a special bath. During Ramadan, the
ninth month of the Muslim calendar, daily
prayers and fasting are obligatory for everyone
except children and the mentally incapacitated.

Muslim parents in Hausa towns and cities
favor an Islamic education for their children.

After circumcision, at the age of seven or nine, boys are placed under the instruction and super-vision of a *malaam* to pursue their studies in the Koran. Many Hausa today follow a mixture of Islam and their traditional beliefs.

▼ DEVIL POSSESSION (*BORI*) ▼

The Hausa believe that it is possible to be possessed by devils. A possessed person must go through a devil-possession ceremony to cure the bad symptoms, usually illness. There are many different kinds of devils, including paramount chiefs, white devils, dust devils, and devils living in the mountains, in the forest, and in the water.

To produce a cure, information must first be secured about which devil or devils might have been offended by what actions of the victim. The devils are also consulted about their inten-tions and what cure is required. Before the actual cleansing ceremony, some ninety-nine different roots of trees are gathered and boiled in a pot, to be served to the victim later.

The ceremony requires the playing of music and the call tunes of the devils with a stringed instrument. A sacrificed chicken is placed on the head of the victim. Then the drummer plays the tunes of the different devils. If contact is estab-lished, the devil is said to take a seat near the sufferer, who generally responds to the proximity of supernatural powers by shivering rhythmically. This is usually a sign that the sufferer has been possessed by the spirit, rendering the person unconscious. The devil can then speak through its victim.

Various festivities are held on the night before the ceremony ends, followed the next morning by feasting, drumming, and dancing. Any left-over food is offered to the devils. The ceremony then ends, and the initiate is now healed and ready to leave as a full member. Disproportionately more women than men experience devil possession.

▼ SPORTS AND LEISURE ▼

Wrestling and boxing are two important leisure activities of the Hausa. Wrestling tends to be more popular in villages in the northern region, rather than in cities or large towns. There is elaborate preparation for a wrestling match. The wrestlers dress differently from others. They wear leather aprons, short or sleeveless shirts, and a cap that could cover the ears. They grow their hair long and sometimes plait it. Some wear rings in one ear and use tobacco leaves and kolanuts to dye their teeth deep red. Belts of leather with attached amulets are also worn for protection. The wrestling clubs are usually made of bamboo sticks.

Becoming a wrestler requires being apprenticed at the age of about fifteen and learning from the older wrestlers. Wrestlers are ranked according to their experience. The most senior are the retired wrestlers of at least thirty years of age, who have shaved their heads as a mark of their retirement. Next are the experienced wrestlers who are about to retire, followed by the promising youths and finally the small boys who carry the bags of their seniors.

Wrestling matches usually are held after the millet harvest, with wrestling teams going on a circuit to neighboring villages. Wrestling competitions between villages begin when the youths of one village go to another and post a public challenge to fight by hanging their wrestling bags on the door of any house in the village. Contests are whole-village affairs, and spectators often travel from distant villages and hamlets. The older retired wrestlers serve as referees. The preliminaries consist of a great deal of showmanship. Drummers beat out the call-tunes of individual wrestlers. This signals them to enter the ring, strut around, and praise themselves. After completing a wrestling circuit, participants are in turn visited by wrestlers from other villages until the end of the harvest season. A wrestling team tours neighboring villages for about a week.

Boxing is engaged in principally by butchers. The distinguishing marks of a boxer are either

Some Hausa Proverbs

Da mugun rawa, gara (gwamma) kin tashi.	A fruitless effort is worse than idleness.
A bar kaza cikin gashinta.	Let sleeping dogs lie.
Nuna sani a kasuwar jahilai wauta ne.	Where ignorance is bliss, it is folly to be wise.
Karamin sani kukumi ne.	A little learning is a dangerous thing.
Gani ya kori ji.	Seeing is believing.
Kowa ya kona runbunsa, ya san inda toka ke kudi ne.	Apparent stupidity can be concealed wisdom.
Wurin barnar giwa ba a kulawa da ta biri.	In the face of serious disaster, small troubles pass unnoticed.
Mugun gatarinka ya fi sari ka ba ni	Your own modest possession is better than dependence on others.
In mutum ya ce zai hadiye gatari rike masa kotar.	Do not try to dissuade the person who is set to attempt the impossible.
Don tuwon gobe a ke wanke tukunya.	Kindness begets kindness.
Maras gaskiya ko cikin ruwa ya yi jibi.	A guilty conscience needs no accuser.
In ka ga gemum dan'uwanka ya kama da wuta shafa wa naka ruwa	When your neighbor's house burns, be careful of your own.

long, plaited hair or a shaved head except around the center. Boxers, like wrestlers, toured neighboring towns where they were fed, but they were usually accompanied only by apprentices rather than a large supporting crowd. Like wrestlers, boxers are classified according to seniority and have juniors to carry their equipment. Boxers are accompanied by drummers, who use small, hourglass-shaped drums, unlike the cylindrical drum used for the wrestlers.

▼ MUSIC AND DANCE ▼

Music is a vital part of Hausa life. Traditionally, Hausa society has resident musicians who are fully supported by their communities. Almost all physical activity is accompanied by particular work songs, praise songs, and the beat of drums.

Drummers travel with trading caravans and also perform for farmers. Women accompany domestic activities with song. During the dry season, young girls entertain themselves at night by singing and dancing. In the past, musicians were also used on the battlefield.

Hausa music can be classified into music for royalty, music for dancing, and music associated with various professional guilds. Most royal music is solely for listening and valued for its lyrics. Most royal musicians are essentially praise singers.

Different guilds have their own songs for various purposes—songs for hunters, for blacksmiths, butchers, and other groups. On page 8 of this book is a Hausa musician playing for the archers' guild during an Independence Day celebration in Nigeria. Musicians and praise singers charge fees, except for religious services or burials. In the special case of naming ceremonies and weddings, praise songs are not usually accompanied by music. Each type of Hausa music is associated with its own instruments, such as drums or wind or string instruments.

A long-standing tradition in Hausaland is a festival of dances performed by "dancing magicians." The festival is an occasion for public showmanship and the performance of magic tricks. It takes place in areas where shared farming is underway. The dancers move from one town to another, accompanied by drummers. Their drums are made of calabash gourds with animal skin stretched over the top. The dancers wear leather bands with charms attached. These charms are meant to protect the dancers from harm and enhance their performance. The drummers of one village or town beat the call tune of a person from their village. This is an invitation for him to do his trick, after his praise song has been recited. These festivals are said to build friendships and solidarity between towns.

▼ HAUSA DRESS ▼

Hausa clothing and design were well known throughout West Africa and had an impact, in particular, on the dress style of the chiefs in Ghana and the general population. The traditional dress of Hausa women had great variety in design, fabric, and amount of embroidery. A

Rulers of the Hausa/Fulani states established by the *jihads* wore robes like this. The finest robes were mostly woven and embroidered by the Nupe. This example bears a design known as "eight knives."

woman's dress typically consists of a wrapper or *madauri*, a blouse or *rigarmata*, a headtie or *fatala*, and a wide blanket or *lullubi*, used to cover the body and head. The degree to which any of these is embroidered depends on the woman's taste and income.

Men have a wider range of dress styles. For formal wear, the use of cloaks or *alkyabba* was reserved for the king, high officials, and the

Chief Imam, the Muslim priest, though permission to wear capes was granted to the heads of guilds on certain public occasions. Trousers could either be very narrow or have very wide legs. Caps and turbans, when worn, varied in color and type of material. Sandals or slippers were usually worn. For nonformal wear, men could choose between long or short trousers and shirt sleeves. The wearing of a cap was necessary only with certain combinations.

▼ BIRTH ▼

Hausa attitude about birth is captured in their saying, "If death has a remedy, then birth is that remedy." The birth process is organized around certain customs. When a husband discovers that his wife is pregnant, he must collect at least a three-month supply of firewood for the hot baths his wife must take after the delivery. The birth is assisted by a midwife. She is responsible for cutting the umbilical cord and attends to the needs of the mother and child for several days, washing the child every morning and evening. Just after the birth, the mother drinks a spicy gruel with potash.

Four days after the birth, the legs and jaw of a cow are prepared both as meat and broth, and are eaten by the mother and various family members. The mother usually weans the child at about two years of age. Because it is thought

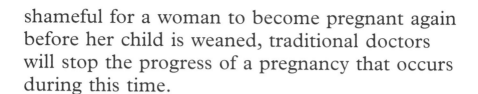

shameful for a woman to become pregnant again
before her child is weaned, traditional doctors
will stop the progress of a pregnancy that occurs
during this time.

▼ NAMING CEREMONY ▼

Seven days after the birth of the child, a naming ceremony is organized. The father must ob-
tain kolanuts to distribute on the day to his and
his wife's parents, friends, and neighbors. He
must also have the front of his house thoroughly
swept and place there carpets and skin mats for
his guests to sit on., He provides an animal—
preferably a bull or ram—to be sacrificed on the
occasion. When the animal is being slaughtered,
the *malaam*, or religious leader, is told the name
for the child. After the sacrifice, the *malaam*
requests all present to offer prayers to Mohammed. He then prays in Arabic and Hausa,
blesses the child, and expresses hopes for a long
life and commitment to the Islamic faith. After
these final prayers, using cash or goods, the father pays the *malaam*, the meat preparers, the
midwife, and the neighbors who assisted with
household help. A barber is then brought for-
ward to perform the final service of shaving the
child's head completely and making any desired
tribal marks. In the evening, the wife entertains
her friends and relatives.

Popular names for males are those of the

twenty-five prophets in the Koran, such as Mohammed, Isa (Jesus), Musa (Moses), Yakubu (Jacob), Yusuru (Joseph), and Dauda (David). Also popular are the names of Mohammed's companions, such as Abubakar and Hamza, and the ninety-nine names of God in the Koran, prefixed by the word "Abdul," which means "servant of," in such names as Abdullahi and Abdulaziz. Girls are often named for some historical Hausa figure such as Amina or Aishatu. Names for male or female children can be chosen by the father without the consent of his wife.

Circumcision of males at the age of seven is required by Islam, although in practice it can be done a few years later. It is usually performed by a trained barber. Circumcision can be carried out either individually or in groups. Circumcision groups live under supervision in the same room, during which they must avoid contact with other boys and the eating of certain foods. The circumcised must sleep on their backs for one to five weeks to promote healing. When they are healed, they are washed, have their heads shaved, and receive a new *bante* or loincloth.

▼ MARRIAGE ▼

Specific rules also govern traditional marriages. Marriage requires demonstration of consent by both parties, the acceptance of responsibility on the part of the husband for providing

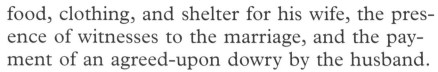

food, clothing, and shelter for his wife, the presence of witnesses to the marriage, and the payment of an agreed-upon dowry by the husband.

Polygamy, the marriage of more than one wife, is permitted in Islam up to a maximum of four wives, provided a man is able to support them and treat them fairly. He is allowed as many concubines (usually slaves) as he can afford.

The marriage of children is accepted by the Hausa. In rural areas, those marrying at a very early age, such as five or six, are expected to be brought up and live in the home of the husband. Under these circumstances, the parents of the boy assume responsibility for the upkeep of both young people. In the view of some Hausa, early marriage encourages marital love and respect, since the girl has not reached the age of defiance (adolescence) at which she might reject her father's choice of a husband.

Such forced marriage, or the father's right to choose a husband for his daughter before puberty, without his wife's or daughter's consent, is acceptable in Islam. Some fathers even assume the right to choose husbands for much older daughters, and even divorced daughters. Other fathers, however, accept some responsibility for the failure of a first marriage and allow more freedom of choice for the second marriage. The Hausa system of marriage is reported to be subject to abuse by parents and to have resulted in a high divorce rate. For example, daughters might be married off to unsuitable or older men for money or prestige. However, the Hausa also have a custom of *sadaka* marriage, whereby a father chooses a poor or learned man for his daughter without the expectation of great financial gain. This type of marriage was also used to marry undesirable daughters to undesirable suitors, including those who already had more than one wife.

▼ DIVORCE ▼

Hausa wives and husbands enjoy different freedoms and follow different procedures for divorce. The wife seeking a divorce has to make a formal application to the court and pay court fees and the costs for serving a summons on her husband. A short delay in the order can be granted by a judge to allow for the possibility of reconciliation. If that occurs, the suit is closed and the husband refunds all expenses incurred by his wife in having brought the suit.

In the absence of reconciliation, the marriage is legally ended. Then the divorced woman goes through a three-month period of waiting called *iddah*. During *iddah*, Islamic law forbids the wife to respond to or accept gifts from other suitors, for this is the final opportunity for the husband and wife to reconcile and resume their marriage. Should there be no reconciliation, the couple is allowed to resume the marriage without a new wedding ceremony. Traditionally, during *iddah,* the wife remained in the marital home and was supported by her husband. More recently, the husband sends his wife back to her parental home without the benefit of material support. Also, the rules regarding new suitors and the offering of gifts are no longer strictly observed.

Unlike his wife, a husband seeking a divorce does not have to initiate a court process. He has the option of simply sending his wife back to her parents, with a written declaration of divorce, followed by a waiting period of three months. If the declaration of divorce is made only once or twice, the husband still has the option of taking his wife back. But on the third time, the divorce is final and the husband can remarry his wife only after she herself has remarried, divorced and completed *iddah.* Custody of children of weaning age or older was usually granted to the husband; whereas children being breast-fed were awarded to the wife. In either case, the father was obliged to provide maintenance for the children.

▼ DEATH AND BURIAL ▼

When a person dies, the place of burial in the communal burial ground is cleared of weeds and a grave is dug. Traditionally, the corpse is laid on its side, in a space about eighteen inches wide and deep, and long enough for the corpse. In rural areas, each household may have its own burial ground at or near a special corner of the house.

The body is prepared by religious washing according to specific religious rules. Various parts are washed first, such as the sexual organs, the head, the face, and the neck. Then the right side of the body down to the ankle is washed before the left side. The body is then wrapped in a cloth called *kubba* and carried to the burial site, where prayers are conducted and verses of the Koran are recited. The face of the corpse is turned eastward toward Mecca.

After a burial, the family of the deceased assemble at home to receive condolences for three days. Alms are given to the poor on behalf of the deceased in the form of food: bean, millet, or corn cakes, and *gumba*, a millet preparation. A period of mourning then begins. A wife can mourn a husband for a maximum of four months and ten days. Out of respect for the deceased during the mourning period, women abstain from dressing their hair or wearing jewelry and cosmetics. They cannot marry during this period.▲

Hausa doorways often receive special decoration, particularly if the homeowner is affluent. This house is in Zaria.

CONCLUSION

THE HAUSA PEOPLE HAVE HAD INTENSE, sustained interaction with their neighbors on all sides. The most important factors behind this interaction were the migration of Saharan peoples from the north; the establishment of various networks of trade; and the political and military ambitions of rival kingdoms and empires. Hausaland, although plagued by internal competition and conflict among its states, and hence not able to become a centralized power, achieved a high degree of social and cultural unity in the region. The spread of Hausa language and the growth of Islam greatly contributed to this achievement. The same is true of the fact that the Hausa themselves were on the move, settling especially in areas to their south and west, where they gained a reputation as excellent traders and soldiers.

For Further Reading

Adamu, M. "The Hausa and Their Neighbors in the Central Sudan," in *The General History of Africa*, vol. 4. Paris: UNESCO, 1984.

—————. *The Hausa Factor in West African History*. Zaria: Ahmadu Bello University Press and Oxford University Press, 1978.

Ajayi, J. F. A., and Crowder, Michael. *A History of West Africa*, vol. 2. New York: Columbia University Press, 1973.

Davidson, Basil, and Buah, F. K. *History of West Africa*. New York: Anchor Books, 1966.

Koslow, Philip. *Hausaland: The Fortress Kingdoms*. New York: Chelsea House Publishers, 1995.

Madauci, Ibraham; Isa, Yahaya; and Daura, Bello. *Hausa Customs*. Zaria: Northern Nigeria Publishing Co., 1968.

Index

ABOUT THE AUTHOR

Dr. Ronald G. Parris is founding Director of the Ralph Bunche Institute of International Studies and the former Chairman of the Department of African, African-American, and Caribbean Studies at William Paterson College. Previously he served at the United Nations Educational, Scientific, and Cultural Organization (UNESCO), Paris, where he was responsible for programs on rural development, international migration, population, and the environment. In that capacity, he traveled widely in Africa, Europe, and the Americas. Dr. Parris was the Covington Visiting Distinguished Professor at Davidson College. He also served on the faculty of New York University and was Dean of the School of the Arts and Sciences at Virginia Union University.

Dr. Parris grew up in Barbados, West Indies, before coming to the United States for his college education. He holds a Ph.D. in Sociology from Yale University. He lives in Montclair, New Jersey.

COMMISSIONING EDITOR: Chukwuma Azuonye, Ph.D.

CONSULTING EDITOR: Gary N. van Wyk, Ph.D.

PHOTO CREDITS: Cover, pp. 8, 23, 24, 26, 28 © Eliot Elisofon, National Museum of African Art, Eliot Elisofon Photographic Archives, Smithsonian Institution; pp. 22, 42, 58 by Herbert M. Cole; pp. 14, 19, 20, 35 © Werner Forman Archive/Art Resource, London/New York; p. 51 © Werner Forman Archive/Art Resource, Wallace Collection, London.

LAYOUT AND DESIGN: Kim Sonsky